88 Garlic Cheese Dip Recipes

(88 Garlic Cheese Dip Recipes - Volume 1)

Jennifer Allen

Copyright: Published in the United States by Jennifer Allen/ © JENNIFER ALLEN

Published on December, 02 2020

All rights reserved. No part of this publication may be reproduced, stored in retrieval system, copied in any form or by any means, electronic, mechanical, photocopying, recording or otherwise transmitted without written permission from the publisher. Please do not participate in or encourage piracy of this material in any way. You must not circulate this book in any format. JENNIFER ALLEN does not control or direct users' actions and is not responsible for the information or content shared, harm and/or actions of the book readers.

In accordance with the U.S. Copyright Act of 1976, the scanning, uploading and electronic sharing of any part of this book without the permission of the publisher constitute unlawful piracy and theft of the author's intellectual property. If you would like to use material from the book (other than just simply for reviewing the book), prior permission must be obtained by contacting the author at author@rosemaryrecipes.com

Thank you for your support of the author's rights.

Content

88 AWESOME GARLIC CHEESE DIP RECIPES 5

1. A Greek Ladys Feta Cheese Dip Recipe 5
2. American Buffalo Wings With Bleu Cheese Dip Recipe 5
3. Anti Dracula Garlic Cheese Dip Recipe 5
4. Avacodo And Goat Cheese Dip Recipe 6
5. BAKED PARMESAN DIP Recipe 6
6. BLUE CHEESE DIP Recipe 7
7. Bacon Cheese Dip Recipe 7
8. Bacon And Garlic Blue Cheese Dip Recipe 7
9. Bacon Cheese Dip Recipe 8
10. Baked Cheese Dip In Sourdough Bread Bowl Recipe 8
11. Beer Cheese Dip Recipe 8
12. Best Ever Blue Cheese Dip Recipe 9
13. Bleu Cheese Dip Recipe 9
14. Blue Cheese Dip Recipe 9
15. Blue Cheese And Bacon First Down Dip Recipe 10
16. Blue Cheese And Shrimp Dip Recipe 10
17. Blue Cheese Bacon Dip Recipe 10
18. Broad Bean And Feta Dip Recipe 11
19. Buffalo Chicken Dip Recipe 11
20. Cheddar Pretzel Dip Recipe 11
21. Cheddar Onion Dip Recipe 12
22. Cheese Olive Dip Recipe 12
23. Cheese And Green Onion Dip With Olive Oil And Lemon With Grilled Pita Recipe 12
24. Cheese N Bean Dip Recipe 13
25. Chili Brie Cheese Dip In Sourdough Round Recipe 13
26. Chokes And Cheese Dip Recipe 13
27. Coca Cola Cheese Dip Recipe 14
28. Cottage Cheese Dip Recipe 14
29. Crab Cheese Dip Recipe 14
30. Cream Cheese Dip Recipe 15
31. Cream Cheese Guacamole Dip Recipe 15
32. Creamy Artichoke Cheese Dip Recipe 15
33. Creamy Bleu Cheese Dipping Sauce Recipe 16
34. Crispy Parmesan Potato Wedges With Lemon Basil Dip Recipe 16
35. Disney Nacho Cheese Dip Copycat Recipe Recipe 16
36. El Azteco Cheese Dip Recipe 17
37. El Steveos Cheese Dip Recipe 17
38. Feta Artichoke Dip Recipe 17
39. Feta Cheese Dip Recipe 17
40. Feta Pine Nut Dip Recipe 18
41. Garlic Feta Cheese Spread Recipe 18
42. HERBED SOUR CREAM BLUE CHEESE DIp Recipe 18
43. HOT FETA ARTICHOKE DIP Recipe . 19
44. Healthier Yogurt Cheese Dip Recipe 19
45. Herb Mix For Cheese Spread Recipe 19
46. High Octane Blue Cheese Dip Recipe 20
47. Hot Artichoke Cheese Spinach Dip Recipe 20
48. Hot Artichoke Parmesan Dip Recipe 20
49. Hot Bacon Cheese Dip Recipe 21
50. Hot Broccoli Cheese Dip Recipe 21
51. Hot Crab And Cheese Dip Recipe 21
52. Hot Fennel Cheese Dip Recipe 22
53. Hot Hot Cheesy Spinach Dip Recipe 22
54. Hot Spinach And Cheese Dip Recipe 22
55. Hot Bacon And Cheese Dip Recipe 23
56. Italian Beer Cheese Dip From Mancinos Recipe 23
57. Kenai Alaska Jalepeno Cheese Dip Recipe 23
58. Mexican Cheese Dip Recipe 24
59. Mexico Chiquito Cheese Dip Recipe 24
60. Mikeys Cheese Dip Recipe 24
61. Mozzarella Dip Recipe 25
62. Muskoka Goat Cheese Dip Recipe 25
63. My Own Mexican Cheese Dip Oolala Recipe 25
64. Oh La La Quick Muffalotta Dip Recipe ... 26
65. Packer Dip Recipe 26
66. Parmesan Artichoke Dip Recipe 27
67. Parmesan Confetti Dip Recipe 27
68. Parmesan Garlic Rosemary Sicily Italian Bread Dip Mix Seasoning Recipe 27
69. Parmesan Salsa Recipe 28
70. Pea Dip With Parmesan Recipe 28
71. Potato Dippers With Jalapeno Cheddar Dip Recipe 28
72. Quick Holiday Cheese Dip Recipe 29
73. Sausage And Cheese Party Dip Recipe 29

74. Sinsinnati Beer Cheese Dip Recipe 30
75. Slow Cooker Cheese Dip Recipe 30
76. Southwestern Cheese Dip Recipe 30
77. Spicey Sausage Cream Cheese Dip Recipe 31
78. Spinach With Feta Cheese Dip Recipe 31
79. String Cheese Sticks With Dipping Sauce Recipe 31
80. Supposedly Wilt Chamberlins Hot Cheese Spinach Dip Recipe 32
81. Three Cheese Spinach Artichoke Dip Recipe 32
82. Vidalia Onion Cheese Dip Recipe 33
83. Warm Blue Cheese Bacon Garlic Dip Recipe 33
84. Warm Blue Cheese Dip Recipe 33
85. Warm Crab Parmesan Dip Recipe 34
86. Warm Crab Spinach And Parmesan Dip Recipe 34
87. Warm Havarti Spinach Dip Recipe 34
88. Zesty Chili Cheese Dip Recipe 35

INDEX 36
CONCLUSION 38

88 Awesome Garlic Cheese Dip Recipes

***

1. A Greek Ladys Feta Cheese Dip Recipe

Serving: 6 | Prep: | Cook: | Ready in:

Ingredients

- 1/2 lb. feta cheese
- 1 pkg. (8 oz) cream cheese, softened
- 1 tbls. milk
- 2 cloves garlic
- 1 tbls. parsley, fresh
- 1/2 tsp. oregano, dried
- 1/2 tsp. thyme, dried
- Lots of black pepper, freshly ground
- Serve with pita chips, bagel chips, or your favorite dippers.

Direction

- Cook time is not chill time
- Put all ingredients into food processor and process until smooth
- Chill

2. American Buffalo Wings With Bleu Cheese Dip Recipe

Serving: 6 | Prep: | Cook: 45mins | Ready in:

Ingredients

- 24 chicken wings disjointed
- 1 stick butter melted
- 8 tablespoons hot pepper sauce
- 1/4 teaspoon cayenne pepper
- 4 tablespoons soy sauce
- 1 cup brown sugar
- 6 cloves garlic minced
- Dip:
- 6 ounce package cream cheese softened
- 1/2 cup sour cream
- 2 tablespoons mayonnaise
- 1/2 teaspoon salt
- 1 teaspoon white pepper
- 4 ounces bleu cheese crumbled

Direction

- Preheat oven to 400.
- Place wings in baking pan.
- In mixing bowl combine remaining ingredients then coat wings on both sides.
- Bake 45 minutes basting frequently.
- Just before serving pour remaining sauce over wings and broil 1 minute.
- In bowl of a food processor combine all dip ingredients except bleu cheese.
- Process until creamy then add bleu cheese but do not process to keep dip chunky.
- Spoon into a bowl and refrigerate until ready to use.

3. Anti Dracula Garlic Cheese Dip Recipe

Serving: 14 | Prep: | Cook: | Ready in:

Ingredients

- 2 (8 oz.) packages cream cheese
- 1/4 cup mayonnaise (real mayo, not Miracle Whip)
- 1/2 cup sour cream
- 1 tbsp fresh parsley, chopped

- 7 or 8 big, fat cloves fresh garlic, minced (i usually use more though -- adjust to your taste)
- 3 tbsp fresh green onion, chopped
- salt and pepper, to taste

Direction

- ***note*** Allow cream cheese to stand at room temperature for 20-30 minutes before making.
- Combine all ingredients and enjoy. :) Serve w/ veggies, crackers, bread, etc. The flavours intensify as it sits so prepare this ahead of time and chill if you want a very intense flavour.

4. Avacodo And Goat Cheese Dip Recipe

Serving: 10 | Prep: | Cook: 20mins | Ready in:

Ingredients

- 2 large avacodos
- 1 large pkg goat cheese (8 oz.)
- 1/4 large red onion fine choped
- 3 cloves garlic fine chopped
- 1 shallot chopped
- 1 tsp cajun spice
- 1 tblspn garlic salt
- 3oz cilantro fine chopped
- sliced almonds
- juice of 1 lime
- fresh ground black pepper
- 2 tblspn olive oil
- (optional 1 hot red chili pepper or more)
- 1 pkg mixed color bell peppers or 3 red bell peppers
- raspberry balsamic vinegar

Direction

- Allow cheese to come to room temp
- Peel and seed avocado and cut to smaller pieces
- Add everything else except bell peppers and balsamic vinegar
- Combine in bowl, mash and mix until a smooth consistency is achieved
- Blanch bell peppers in boiling water for 2 min
- Slice and core peppers
- Place pepper strips on cookie sheet
- Roast in oven 20 min at 400
- Remove from oven drizzle with raspberry balsamic vinegar
- Serve with your favourite crackers
- A little dip a little pepper.

5. BAKED PARMESAN DIP Recipe

Serving: 12 | Prep: | Cook: 30mins | Ready in:

Ingredients

- 1 package (10 oz.) frozen chopped spinach, thawed, or 1 13.75 oz. can water-packed artichoke hearts, drained and chopped
- 1 cup reduced-fat or regular mayonnaise
- 1 package (3 oz.) cream cheese
- 1 onion (6 oz.), peeled and minced
- 1 clove garlic, pressed or minced
- 1 cup plus 2 tbsp. Shredded parmesan cheese
- 1/8 tsp. pepper
- 1/2 tsp. paprika
- 2 Artisan baguettes (8 oz.), thinly sliced

Direction

- Squeeze spinach to remove liquid. With a mixer, beat spinach, mayonnaise, cream cheese, onion, garlic, 1 cup of the parmesan cheese, and pepper until thoroughly combined.
- Mound mixture in a 3- to 4-cup baking dish. Sprinkle evenly with 2 tbsp. parmesan cheese and paprika.
- Bake in a 350° oven until hot in centre and lightly browned on top, 25 to 30 minutes.
- Serve hot to spread on baguette slices.

6. BLUE CHEESE DIP Recipe

Serving: 10 | Prep: | Cook: | Ready in:

Ingredients

- 1 C mayonnaise
- 1/2 C sour cream
- 1 T lemon juice
- 1 T white vinegar
- 1/2 C crumbled blue cheese
- 2 T onion (minced)
- 1 clove Garlic (minced)
- 1/4 C fresh chopped parsley
- salt and pepper to taste

Direction

- Blend all ingredients and chill for at least 2 hours (overnight is better!) to allow the flavours to meld.
- Serve with your favourite crackers and/or veggies.
- Makes about 2 cups.

7. Bacon Cheese Dip Recipe

Serving: 16 | Prep: | Cook: 10mins | Ready in:

Ingredients

- 4 slices bacon
- 1 (8oz) package cream cheese, softened
- 1/3 cup light mayo
- 6 oz shredded swiss cheese
- 1/4 cup parmesan cheese
- 2 green onions, finely chopped
- 4 buttery round crackers, crushed
- garlic powder to taste

Direction

- Cook bacon until brown and crisp
- Drain, crumble and set aside
- In a small bowl, mix the cream cheese with mayo until smooth
- Stir in Swiss cheese, parm, onions and bacon
- Add desired amount of garlic powder
- Microwave for 2 minutes
- Remove and stir well
- Return to microwave and cook 2-4 minutes more
- Sprinkle crushed crackers on top
- Serve warm with crackers

8. Bacon And Garlic Blue Cheese Dip Recipe

Serving: 12 | Prep: | Cook: 35mins | Ready in:

Ingredients

- 8 slices bacon
- 2 cloves garlic, minced
- 1 (8 ounce) package cream cheese, softened
- 1/4 cup milk
- 4 ounces blue cheese, crumbled
- 2 tablespoons chopped fresh chives

Direction

- Preheat oven to 350 degrees F.
- Cook bacon over medium high heat until evenly brown. Remove bacon from skillet, drain on paper towels and crumble.
- Place garlic in hot bacon grease. Cook and stir until soft, about 1 minute. Remove from heat.
- Place cream cheese and milk in a medium bowl. Beat with an electric mixer until blended. Stir in bacon, garlic, blue cheese and chives. Transfer mixture to a medium baking dish.
- Bake 30 minutes, or until lightly browned.

9. Bacon Cheese Dip Recipe

Serving: 10 | Prep: | Cook: 60mins | Ready in:

Ingredients

- 1 two lb. loaf of round bread (preferred pumpernickle or rye)
- Cut off lid and hollow out inside.
- 1 lb. of bacon (fried and crumbled)
- 1 cup of grated sharp cheddar cheese
- 1 cup of monterey jack shredded-sometimes sub jack with jalapeno
- 1 cup of parmesan
- 1 small grated onion
- 1 large glove of garlic minced
- 1 cup of mayonnaise

Direction

- Combine bacon, cheese, onion, garlic and mayonnaise.
- Mix well. (Can add a dash of hot sauce, if desired.)
- Spoon into hollowed out bread.
- Top with reserved lid.
- Double wrap in foil.
- Bake one hour with lid at 350 degrees.
- Serve with breadsticks, bread cubes and sturdy chips for dipping.

10. Baked Cheese Dip In Sourdough Bread Bowl Recipe

Serving: 8 | Prep: | Cook: 75mins | Ready in:

Ingredients

- 1 round sourdough bread, hollowed out (10 in.)
- 1 can artichokes, not marinated, chopped
- 1 cup cheddar cheese, shredded
- 1 clove garlic, minced
- 1 cup mayonnaise
- 1 cup monterey jack cheese, shredded
- 1 small onion, finely chopped
- 1 cup parmesan cheese, grated
- .

Direction

- Preheat oven to 350
- Hollow out sourdough bread (save insides)
- Mix rest of ingredients together
- Put mixture into bread
- Put lid back on bread
- Bake 1 1/4 hours
- Cube bread and place around bowl

11. Beer Cheese Dip Recipe

Serving: 46 | Prep: | Cook: | Ready in:

Ingredients

- 1-8 ounce package sharp cheddar cheese, shredded
- 4 ounces cream cheese, softened
- 1 garlic clove, minced
- 1 tablespoon worcestershire sauce
- 1 teaspoon horseradish, grated
- 1/2 teaspoon dry mustard
- 1/4 teaspoon ground red pepper
- 1/4 cup beer (darker as in Bass, Guinness or other stout)
- salt and pepper to taste
- pretzels, crusty bread and/or crackers to serve

Direction

- In a bowl, beat cheese together with an electric mixer until smooth.
- Add garlic, Worcestershire sauce, horseradish, dry mustard and red pepper.
- Beat well until thoroughly blended.
- Gradually add beer until well blended.
- Taste...and salt and pepper to your liking if needed.
- Cover and chill for 1 hour before serving.

- Serve with crusty bread, pretzels and/or crackers.

12. Best Ever Blue Cheese Dip Recipe

Serving: 10 | Prep: | Cook: 5mins | Ready in:

Ingredients

- 2 Tbs olive oil
- 4 cloves of garlic minced
- 3 shallots minced
- 1/2 tsp mustard powder
- 1 1/2 cups sour cream
- 1/2 cup Greek yoghurt
- 2 Tbs real mayonisse
- 1 3/4 cup crumbled blue cheese
- Garnish
- 1 Tbs fresh minced parsley
- pinch paprika

Direction

- Over medium heat, add oil and garlic, shallots and mustard powder. Sautéed until shallots and garlic browned and tender about 4 or 5 minutes.
- Do not let burn
- Remove from skillet and let cool 5 minutes
- Stir in everything else except garnish
- Chill at least 30 minutes
- When serving sprinkle with parsley and paprika
- Serve with hot wings or Buffalo wings

13. Bleu Cheese Dip Recipe

Serving: 10 | Prep: | Cook: | Ready in:

Ingredients

- 2 1/2 oz bleu cheese crumbles
- 3 green onions, finely chopped
- 1 cup sour cream (can use light or fat free)
- 3 Tbs mayo (can use light...I wouldn't use fat free)
- 1 Tbs worcestershire sauce
- garlic powder

Direction

- Mash onions and cheese together.
- Add sour cream and blend with fork
- Add mayo, Worcestershire sauce, and blend
- Add sprinkle garlic powder to taste.
- Refrigerate at least an hour.
- **This would also make a delicious "stuffing" for chicken or steak!
- ***Enjoy!

14. Blue Cheese Dip Recipe

Serving: 8 | Prep: | Cook: | Ready in:

Ingredients

- 1 cup mayonnaise
- 1 cup sour cream
- 4 green onions, finely chopped
- 2 tablespoons dried parsley
- 4 ounces blue cheese, crumbled
- garlic salt to taste

Direction

- 1. In a medium bowl, mix mayonnaise, sour cream, green onions, dried parsley, blue cheese and garlic salt. Cover and chill in the refrigerator until serving.

15. Blue Cheese And Bacon First Down Dip Recipe

Serving: 10 | Prep: | Cook: 20mins | Ready in:

Ingredients

- 8 slices bacon, chopped
- 1 tablespoon minced garlic
- 2 (8-oz.) packages cream cheese, softened
- 1 cup (4-oz.) crumbled blue cheese
- 1/3 cup cream
- 2 tablespoons minced green onions
- 1/4 cup toasted walnut pieces

Direction

- Cook bacon in skillet until crisp, stirring often. Remove from skillet and drain.
- Add garlic to skillet and sauté over low heat for 1 minute.
- Combine cream cheese and cream in food processor bowl or mixer and blend until smooth. Stir in bacon, garlic, crumbled cheese and green onions.
- Portion dip in medium baking dish; bake in preheated 350°F oven for 20 minutes. Garnish with toasted walnuts.
- Serve warm dip with kettle cooked potato chips.
- COOKS NOTE: Better-for-You Variation: This dip is also great served with fresh veggie sticks such as red and orange bell peppers, celery and baby carrots.
- COOKS NOTE: For added convenience, dip can be made ahead, held chilled and baked right before serving (be sure to portion the dip in the container that it will be baked in before refrigerating).

16. Blue Cheese And Shrimp Dip Recipe

Serving: 12 | Prep: | Cook: | Ready in:

Ingredients

- 12 oz jarred refrigerated light or regular blue cheese dressing
- 1 (3.53-oz.) drained can or pouch of small cocktail shrimp
- 4 green onions, thinly sliced
- 1 1/2 cloves garlic, minced (roasted optional)
- 1/4 teaspoon each: celery seed, dried thyme, ground mustard, cayenne pepper, white pepper and hot pepper sauce
- crackers or fresh vegetables

Direction

- In a bowl, combine dressing and shrimp and all remaining dip ingredients; (For the blue cheese lovers in your household, add crumbled blue cheese to this dip.) mix well. Cover and chill for at least 2 hours. Serve with crackers or fresh vegetables.

17. Blue Cheese Bacon Dip Recipe

Serving: 12 | Prep: | Cook: 15mins | Ready in:

Ingredients

- 7 bacon slices, chopped
- 2 cloves garlic, minced
- 2 (8 oz.) packages cream cheese, softened
- 1/3 cup half-and-half
- 4 oz. crumbled blue cheese
- 2 Tbs chopped fresh chives
- 3 Tbs chopped walnuts, toasted
- flatbread/assorted crackers

Direction

- Cook chopped bacon in skillet over med-high heat, 10 minutes or until crisp. Drain bacon, and set aside. Add minced garlic to skillet, and sauté 1 minutes.
- Beat cream cheese at medium speed with electric mixer until smooth. Add half-and-half, beating until combined. Stir to combine

- bacon, garlic, blue cheese, and chives. Spoon into 4 (1 cup) baking dishes
- Bake 350 degrees for 15 minutes, or until golden and bubbly. Sprinkle top with walnuts. Enjoy!

18. Broad Bean And Feta Dip Recipe

Serving: 6 | Prep: | Cook: 10mins | Ready in:

Ingredients

- 4 wholemeal Lebanese breads
- 2 cups broad beans, fresh is better but frozen is fine
- 100g marinated feta cheese
- 2 serrano chillies, deseeded and finely sliced
- 100g ricotta cheese
- 1 garlic clove, crushed
- extra virgin olive oil, to serve
- smoked paprika, hot variety

Direction

- Place the Lebanese breads on 2 oven trays and lightly brush them with some of the olive oil, on both sides. Bake in the oven, turning occasionally, until crisp and lightly coloured.
- Remove from oven and set aside.
- Cook the broad beans in a large saucepan of salted boiling water for 5 minutes or until tender.
- Refresh them under cold running water, drain well and peel.
- Place the broad beans, feta, ricotta, chilli and garlic in the bowl of a food processor and process until almost smooth.
- Transfer to a serving bowl. Drizzle with oil and sprinkle with paprika.
- Break the Lebanese breads into large pieces and serve with the broad bean dip.

19. Buffalo Chicken Dip Recipe

Serving: 20 | Prep: | Cook: 45mins | Ready in:

Ingredients

- 2 (10 ounce) cans chunk chicken, drained
- 3/4 C. Frank's Red Hot Sauce
- 1 clove garlic, smashed
- 2 (8 ounce) packages cream cheese, softened
- 1/2 cup Ranch dressing
- 1/2 cup blue cheese dressing
- 1/2 cup crumbled blue cheese
- 1 tsp. Old Bay seasoning
- 1 1/2 cups shredded cheddar cheese

Direction

- Heat chicken and hot sauce in a skillet over medium heat, until heated through. Add garlic. Stir in cream cheese and ranch/Blue cheese dressing. Cook, stirring until well blended and warm. Add blue cheese and Old Bay, stirring to combine. Add half of the shredded cheddar cheese, stirring again. Transfer the mixture to a slow cooker. Sprinkle the remaining cheese over the top, cover, and cook on Low setting until hot and bubbly.
- Serve with celery, tortilla chips, and crackers.

20. Cheddar Pretzel Dip Recipe

Serving: 2 | Prep: | Cook: 5mins | Ready in:

Ingredients

- 8 ounces sharp cheddar cheese, grated
- 3 cloves garlic, peeled
- 1 teaspoon salt
- 2 ounces cream cheese, softened
- 2 tablespoons unsalted butter, softened
- 1 tablespoon Dijon mustard
- 2 tablespoons yellow mustard

Direction

- Mince garlic with salt. In a bowl, combine garlic mixture and cream cheese. Mix until smooth.
- Add shredded Cheddar cheese and mix, or blend in a food processor until smooth.
- Add butter and mustards and mix again until smooth. Scrape down the sides of the bowl and mix or blend one more time.
- Serve at room temperature or slightly warmed.

21. Cheddar Onion Dip Recipe

Serving: 8 | Prep: | Cook: 5mins | Ready in:

Ingredients

- 1 lg. vidalia onion, trimmed and grated(1c)
- 8 oz. sharpcheddar cheese, grated
- 1pkg.(8oz) light cream cheese
- 1tsp garlic powder
- 1/4tsp ground cayenne pepper
- chopped scallion.for garnish(optional)
- assorted crackers

Direction

- In med-size cast iron or oven safe skillet, combine onion, cheeses, garlic powder and cayenne pepper. Cook over grill heated to medium heat, stirring till cheese is melted, about 5 mins. Garnish with scallions, if desired. Serve with crackers.

22. Cheese Olive Dip Recipe

Serving: 8 | Prep: | Cook: | Ready in:

Ingredients

- 2 cups cottage cheese
- 1 8 oz package cream cheese
- 3/4 cup dairy sour cream
- 1 tbsp grated onion
- 1/4 tsp garlic salt
- 1/2 cup chopped ripe olives

Direction

- Combine cottage cheese, cream cheese, sour cream, onion and garlic salt; beat until well blended. Add olives. Chill. Serve with assorted crackers or potato chips.

23. Cheese And Green Onion Dip With Olive Oil And Lemon With Grilled Pita Recipe

Serving: 4 | Prep: | Cook: 2mins | Ready in:

Ingredients

- 12 green onions, green part only, grilled and chopped, plus additional thinly sliced green onions, for garnish
- 1/4 cup extra-virgin olive oil, plus additional for grilling pitas
- 2 tablespoons fresh lemon juice
- 2 teaspoons finely chopped lemon zest
- Salt and freshly ground pepper
- 2 cloves garlic
- 1 pound feta cheese, crumbled
- 8 pocketless pitas

Direction

- Place grilled green onions, oil, lemon juice, and zest in a food processor and process until smooth.
- Add the feta and garlic and process until combined and smooth. Scrape the mixture into a bowl and garnish with the additional sliced green onions.
- Heat grill or broiler to high.
- Brush the pitas with the remaining oil and season with salt and pepper, to taste.
- Grill or broil for 1 minute per side or until lightly golden brown.

- Remove from the grill and cut each pita into eighths. Serve with the feta dip.

24. Cheese N Bean Dip Recipe

Serving: 4 | Prep: | Cook: | Ready in:

Ingredients

- 4 garlic cloves
- 15 oz canned butter beans
- 3/4 cup fat-free cream cheese
- 1 rosemary sprig
- 1 tsp table salt
- 1/4 tsp black pepper

Direction

- Preheat the oven to 350°F.
- Place the garlic cloves on a square of foil, add 2 tsp. water and make a little parcel.
- Roast for about 15 minutes towards the top of the oven, or until the cloves are soft.
- Cool, then squeeze out the softened pulp into a food processor.
- Tip the lima beans into the processor and add the cheese and rosemary.
- Blend until smooth.
- Season to taste with salt and pepper.

25. Chili Brie Cheese Dip In Sourdough Round Recipe

Serving: 8 | Prep: | Cook: 30mins | Ready in:

Ingredients

- 1 round loaf sourdough bread
- 8 ounce wheel brie cheese
- 1 tablespoon butter softened
- 1 teaspoon chili powder
- 1/2 teaspoon dry ground mustard
- 1/2 teaspoon garlic powder
- 1/2 teaspoon granulated sugar

Direction

- Preheat oven to 350.
- Combine spices and sugar then set aside.
- Cut circle in top of bread and remove bread centre to make room for brie.
- Spread butter in bread then sprinkle with 2 teaspoons spice mixture.
- With knife make 2" cuts around edge of bread at 1" intervals.
- Remove rind from brie and place in bread then sprinkle brie with remaining spice.
- Replace top of bread then bake on baking sheet for 25 minutes.
- To serve remove bread top and break into bite size pieces then dip bread pieces in hot brie.

26. Chokes And Cheese Dip Recipe

Serving: 8 | Prep: | Cook: 15mins | Ready in:

Ingredients

- 1 Cup mayonnaise
- 1 can diced green chiles
- 1 can artichoke hearts (5-7 count, drained) cut into bite sized pieces
- 1 Cup Kraft three cheese blend (in shaker) can use parm (reserve 4 tbsp)
- 1/4-1/2 Cup sour cream
- 1/4 tsp chopped/minced garlic (more if you like)
- 1/2 tsp horseradish
- salt and pepper to taste

Direction

- Mix together in an oven/microwave safe container (can use a round loaf of bread that has been cored with room for the filling).
- Microwave for 5 minutes.
- Top with remaining cheese.

- Bake in a 300oF oven until top is brown.

27. Coca Cola Cheese Dip Recipe

Serving: 10 | Prep: | Cook: | Ready in:

Ingredients

- Coca-Cola® cheese Dip
- 12 ounces grated cheddar cheese
- 4 ounces Roquefort cheese -- crumbled
- 1 clove garlic -- pressed
- 3/4 cup Coca-Cola® -- divided
- 2 tablespoons soft margarine
- 1 tablespoon grated onion
- 1 1/2 teaspoons worcestershire sauce
- 1 teaspoon dry mustard
- 1/4 teaspoon salt
- 1/8 teaspoon Tabasco® sauce

Direction

- Place shredded cheddar into a large mixing bowl. Add crumbled
- Roquefort.
- Press garlic into bowl. Add 1/2 cup of the cola. Add margarine, onion, Worcestershire, dry mustard, salt and Tabasco. Beat at low speed until blended. Gradually add the remaining Coke; beat on high until fairly smooth and light.
- Pack in a covered container. Chill a few hours or overnight. Dip keeps well for a week or more. Makes about 3 cups.
- "Originally printed in the Philadelphia Inquirer, date unknown"

28. Cottage Cheese Dip Recipe

Serving: 12 | Prep: | Cook: | Ready in:

Ingredients

- 1 ctn cottage cheese
- 1 (3 oz) package cream cheese, softened
- 1 tsp worcestershire sauce
- 1 T grated onion
- 2T salad dressing/Miracle Whip
- garlic salt to taste

Direction

- Mix all ingredients well and let stand overnight.
- Serve with crackers or chips.

29. Crab Cheese Dip Recipe

Serving: 4 | Prep: | Cook: 30mins | Ready in:

Ingredients

- 1/2 cup light mayoniae
- 1 pkg 8 oz. light cream cheese softened
- 2 tablespoons skim milk
- 4 scallions sliced
- 1 tbs lemon juice
- 1 tsp. red hot sauce
- 1 tsp. Woorcherstershire sauce
- 1/2 tsp garlic salt
- 1/2 cup grated parmeasan cheese
- 1 lb. lump crab meat picked over to remove cartilage
- 1/4 cup parsely chopped
- {May omit crab and use Shrimp}

Direction

- Heat oven to 350 degrees spray a 6 oz. cup shallow baking dish with non-stick cooking spray and set aside
- In a large bowl stir together mayonnaise, cream cheese, Milk scallions ,lemon juice, red pepper sauce Worcestershire sauce, Garlic salt and 1/4 cup parmesan cheese until smooth
- Gently stir in crab meat to keep from breaking up to finely spoon mixture evenly into baking dish

- Sprinkle remaining parmesan cheese over top crab mixture
- Bake 350 for 30 minutes until lightly brown let stand 5 minutes
- Sprinkle chopped Parsley over top serve warm with your favourite dip chip.
- Was given to me by a friend who clipped it out of a magazine

30. Cream Cheese Dip Recipe

Serving: 10 | Prep: | Cook: | Ready in:

Ingredients

- 2 packages of cream cheese
- 1 TBS basil (fresh is better)
- 2 TBS olive oil
- 3 cloves of garlic
- 1 cup Chopped fresh parsley

Direction

- Place 2 packages of room temperature (easier to mix) cream cheese in a serving bowl.
- Using a garlic press, crush the 3 cloves of garlic and put in with cream cheese.
- Add basil, olive oil, and parsley. Using a stiff spoon mix until well blended.
- Chill for about 20 minutes or longer in the refrigerator.
- Can be served on crackers, in celery sticks, or placed as a dip.

31. Cream Cheese Guacamole Dip Recipe

Serving: 4 | Prep: | Cook: | Ready in:

Ingredients

- 8 oz pkg cream cheese (softened)
- 2 avocados, peeled and mashed
- 1/4 cup finely chopped onion
- 1 Tbs lemon juice
- 1/2 tsp salt
- 1/4 tsp garlic salt
- 1/4 tsp hot sauce
- 1 cup diced tomato

Direction

- Combine all ingredients, except tomato and mix well
- Carefully stir in tomato
- Serve with tortilla chips

32. Creamy Artichoke Cheese Dip Recipe

Serving: 12 | Prep: | Cook: 60mins | Ready in:

Ingredients

- 1 jar of artichoke hearts (drained and rinsed and coarsely chopped)
- 2 cups of mayonnaise
- 3 tbsp of unsalted butter
- 1 12 oz package of finely shred parmesean cheese
- 1 12 oz package of finely shred mozerella cheese
- 2 tbsp of garlic powder

Direction

- Butter the inside of a crock pot.
- Add in artichoke hearts, mayo, garlic powder, butter cubes, parmesan cheese and mozzarella cheeses.
- Stir and bake in your crockpot on medium for 1 hour then turn the heat on low and keep simmering for as long as you wish.
- This ooey-gooey cheesy dip is delicious with French bread crisps or pita.

33. Creamy Bleu Cheese Dipping Sauce Recipe

Serving: 6 | Prep: | Cook: | Ready in:

Ingredients

- 1 cup mayonnaise
- 1 cup sour cream
- 1/4 cup or more crumbled bleu cheese
- 2 spring onions, sliced
- 2 garlic cloves, minced
- 1 tablespoon lemon juice
- a dash or 2 of Tobasco Sauce
- Note: Easily doubled.

Direction

- Cream mayonnaise and sour cream well.
- Add crumbled blue cheese followed by spring onions, garlic, lemon juice and Tabasco sauce.
- Mix well.

34. Crispy Parmesan Potato Wedges With Lemon Basil Dip Recipe

Serving: 12 | Prep: | Cook: 60mins | Ready in:

Ingredients

- potato WEDGES:
- 2 - 3 lbs potatoes
- EVOO
- coarse salt
- cracked black pepper
- Grated Parmesan
- DIP:
- 1.5 c Kraft Mayo
- 4 garlic cloves
- 1 T lemon juice
- handful fresh green basil
- handful fresh opal basil
- salt and pepper

Direction

- POTATO WEDGES:
- Preheat oven to 450
- Cut potatoes into thick wedges, (slice into bowl of ice water)
- Remove potatoes from water and place in large Ziploc baggie
- Drizzle with EVOO and seasonings
- Shake
- Pour onto baking sheet and bake 1 hour, or until done and edges are crispy
- DIP:
- Peel, crush, and chop garlic
- Tear both types of basil into small pieces
- Stir garlic, basil, and lemon into mayo
- Salt & Pepper to taste
- Transfer to serving bowl
- Cover with plastic wrap and chill until serving. (I make the dip, and let it chill while potatoes are baking, pull it out of the fried as soon as the potatoes are done).

35. Disney Nacho Cheese Dip Copycat Recipe Recipe

Serving: 15 | Prep: | Cook: 10mins | Ready in:

Ingredients

- 1/2 pound provolone cheese, grated
- 1/2 pound American cheese, grated
- 3/4 cup heavy cream
- 8 ounces cream cheese
- 1/4 teaspoon garlic powder
- 3/4 teaspoon Worcestershire
- 1/8 teaspoon cayenne
- 1/8 teaspoon yellow food coloring

Direction

- Melt provolone in top of double boiler over boiling water.
- Add American cheese and stir in cream.
- Add cream cheese and stir until all is melted.

- Remove from heat; whip in seasonings and food colouring.
- Transfer to crockpot, and keep warm on lowest setting.
- Serve warm with crackers, chips, or veggies.

36. El Azteco Cheese Dip Recipe

Serving: 8 | Prep: | Cook: 30mins | Ready in:

Ingredients

- 1 cup cottage cheese
- 1/2 cup sour cream
- 2 ounces monterey jack cheese, grated
- 2 ounces muenster cheese, grated
- fresh garlic, crushed
- 2 jalapeno peppers, minced
- 2 tablespoons minced green onion
- tortilla chips

Direction

- Combine cottage cheese, sour cream and cheeses
- Add garlic, peppers and green onion; mix well.
- Refrigerate for at least 30 minutes to allow flavours to blend.
- Serve with tortilla chips.

37. El Steveos Cheese Dip Recipe

Serving: 10 | Prep: | Cook: | Ready in:

Ingredients

- 1 Tub sour cream
- 1 Tub small curd cottage cheese
- +- 1 Cup/ Package Shredded Monteray Jack cheese
- (Jack/Sharp Mix works fine too)
- 3 Tablespoons garlic salt
- 3-5 jalapeno peppers-chopped
- 1 Bunch scallions/green onions, chopped

Direction

- Just mix it all together and refrigerate, serve with tortilla chips. Be careful chopping the peppers up.

38. Feta Artichoke Dip Recipe

Serving: 46 | Prep: | Cook: 30mins | Ready in:

Ingredients

- 1 minced clove of garlic
- 1 14 oz can of drained artichoke hearts, chopped
- 1 2 oz jar of diced pimentos, drained
- 8 oz of crumbled feta cheese
- 1 c of mayonnaise
- 1/2 c of shredded parmesan cheese
- 3 chopped green onions (optional)
- 1 chopped tomatoe (optional)

Direction

- Let's start by preheating your oven at 350 F
- Grab you large mixing bowl and stir in all the ingredients.
- Take the mixture and pour it into a pie pan.
- You want to bake it for about 20-25 minutes or until it's slightly brown.
- If you want a little colour you could add some tomatoes or even onions on top.
- Goes great with tortilla chips, pita bread, crackers and a bagel.

39. Feta Cheese Dip Recipe

Serving: 8 | Prep: | Cook: | Ready in:

Ingredients

- 1/2 lb. feta cheese, crumbled
- 1.5 C plain yogurt
- 1 C sour cream
- 3 T chopped garlic (more or less - adjust to taste)
- pepper
- pita bread, or rounds

Direction

- In a blender, blend all ingredients (except pita bread) on low-medium until smooth (but not watery)
- Serve with pita bread
- I use all low-fat ingredients to make this healthier. I also use minced garlic if I do not have fresh on hand. I also prefer whole-wheat pita bread.

40. Feta Pine Nut Dip Recipe

Serving: 2 | Prep: | Cook: | Ready in:

Ingredients

- 1 8 oz. container whipped cream cheese
- 1/2 cup plain non-fat yogurt
- 3 tbsp. toasted pine nuts
- 2 tbsp. chopped fresh basil
- 1 clove garlic, minced
- 7 oz. feta cheese, crumbled
- 1/3 cup oil packed sun-dried tomatoes, chopped

Direction

- Place cream cheese, yogurt, pine nuts, basil and garlic in a food processor. Blend until well combined using on/off turns. Add the feta and sun-dried tomatoes and blend again using on/off turns until blended but still chunky. Serve with pita chips, tortilla chips or celery.

41. Garlic Feta Cheese Spread Recipe

Serving: 0 | Prep: | Cook: 10mins | Ready in:

Ingredients

- 4 oz. feta cheese
- 4 oz. cream cheese
- 1/3 cup mayonnaise
- 4 cloves garlic, minced
- 1/4 teaspoon basil
- 1/4 teaspoon oregano
- 1/8 teaspoon dill weed
- 1/8 teaspoon thyme

Direction

- Place all ingredients in food processor with chopping blade and process until smooth, about 1 minute.
- Cover and refrigerate.
- Delicious however you serve it; on crackers, stuffed in celery, as a dip on a raw veggie tray, scooped up with pita chips. You can't beat it!

42. HERBED SOUR CREAM BLUE CHEESE DIp Recipe

Serving: 2 | Prep: | Cook: | Ready in:

Ingredients

- 1 cup sour cream
- 8 oz Philadelphia cream cheese, softened
- 1/3 cup blue cheese (or blue cheese crumbles)
- 2 tablespoons fresh chives or scallions, minced
- 2 tablespoons fresh parsley, minced
- 1 tablespoon fresh herbs (thyme, rosemary, basil, oregano)
- 2 teaspoons fresh garlic, finely minced
- 1 teaspoon Mrs. Dash (optional)
- 1/4 teaspoon red pepper flakes
- 1/4 teaspoon cracked black pepper

- Allow cream cheese to sit at room temperature for 20-30 minutes before using.

Direction

- In a medium bowl, beat cream cheese using a hand mixer until soft. Add sour cream, blue cheese, and remaining ingredients, mixing well.
- Cover and refrigerate one hour before serving.
- Serving Suggestion:
- Serve accompanied by tortilla chips, celery sticks and cucumber strips, lemon and tomato wedges and a small bowl of hot sauce. Sprinkle vegetables with celery or sea salt and pepper

43. HOT FETA ARTICHOKE DIP Recipe

Serving: 10 | Prep: | Cook: 40mins | Ready in:

Ingredients

- 14 OZ. artichoke hearts-CHOPPED
- 1 C. MAYO
- 1 garlic clove, LARGE, MINCED
- 2 OZ. pimentos-CHOPPED
- 8 OZ. feta cheese-CRUMBLED

Direction

- COMBINE ALL INGREDIENTS
- PUT IN 1 QUART CASSEROLE
- BAKE AT 350 FOR 30-40 MINUTES, OR UNTIL GOLDEN BROWN
- EAT WITH CHIPS, CRACKERS OR CRUSTY BREAD

44. Healthier Yogurt Cheese Dip Recipe

Serving: 8 | Prep: | Cook: |Ready in:

Ingredients

- •4 tablespoons whipped cream cheese or reduced-fat cream cheese
- •10 ounces 2% Fage Greek yogurt
- •2 tablespoons parmesan cheese
- •2 teaspoons dried chives
- •3 cloves garlic, minced
- •1 tablespoon chopped onion
- Serve with crisp, lowfat crackers or crudite

Direction

- Combine all ingredients and blend well with a spoon.
- .Refrigerate for 12 hours or overnight, allowing flavours to marry. Serve with crudité or crisp, low-fat crackers.

45. Herb Mix For Cheese Spread Recipe

Serving: 4 | Prep: | Cook: |Ready in:

Ingredients

- 10 t dried marjoram
- 15 t dried chives
- 15/8 t granulated garlic (or garlic powder)
- 6 t thyme
- 1 1/2 t caraway

Direction

- Mix the ingredients together, then use 1.5 T of the total for every 8 oz. of cheese. The classic would call for just cream cheese, but I like 8 oz. of cream cheese and 4 oz. of soft goat cheese with enough herb mix to accommodate.

- Whatever you use, allow it to sit and blend in the fridge for a day, and preferably leave out for a few hours before serving so it spreads easily.

46. High Octane Blue Cheese Dip Recipe

Serving: 6 | Prep: | Cook: | Ready in:

Ingredients

- 8 oz. cream cheese
- 8 oz. Crumbled blue cheese
- 1- med. onion, I use a spanish onion
- 6-10 fresh garlic cloves

Direction

- This dip is to be prepared using a blender
- I cut the block of cream cheese into 8 pieces because it is so hard to get this mixture "flowing" in the blender especially if you don't do this
- Don't place it all in at once, add some garlic, add some, onion, blue cheese, cream cheese until all comes together in a thick dip consistency.
- This dip is good right away, but best if refrigerated overnight.
- This dip is either loved or hated :)

47. Hot Artichoke Cheese Spinach Dip Recipe

Serving: 4 | Prep: | Cook: 25mins | Ready in:

Ingredients

- 1 (6.25 oz) jar marinated artichokes (drained)
- 1 (10 oz.) package frozen chopped spinach (thawed and drained
- very well)
- 1/2 teaspoon minced garlic
- 1/3 cup grated romano cheese
- 1/4 cup grated parmesan cheese
- 1 cup shredded mozzarella cheese
- 1/3 cup cream or half and half
- 1/2 cup sour cream

Direction

- In food processor blend artichokes, Romano cheese, garlic and parmesan cheese for about 1 - 1 1/2 minutes.
- Artichokes and cheeses should be minced, but should not be pasty.
- In a mixing bowl add drained spinach, cream, sour cream, and mozzarella.
- Stir well.
- Spoon into mixing bowl mixture from food processor.
- Blend all ingredients.
- Mixture should have a medium thick consistency.
- Spray an oven proof shallow serving dish.
- Pour artichoke mixture into baking dish and bake for 20 - 25 minutes at 350F degrees.
- Artichoke dip should be a little bubbly and cheese melted through.
- Remove from oven and serve with your favourite heated tortilla chips, sour cream and salsa.

48. Hot Artichoke Parmesan Dip Recipe

Serving: 8 | Prep: | Cook: 30mins | Ready in:

Ingredients

- 2 cans artichoke hearts, drained
- 1 cup mayonnaise
- 1 cup grated parmesan cheese (freshly grated if possible)
- 2 cloves of garlic
- 1/4 tsp cayenne pepper

- salt to taste

Direction

- Preheat oven to 350F
- Either chop artichoke hearts and garlic finely or grind them in a food processor.
- In a large bowl combine all ingredients.
- Place in a 1 quart baking dish.
- Sprinkle with a little more cayenne.
- Bake about 30 minutes until the top browns.
- Serve the "traditional" way with wheat thins.

49. Hot Bacon Cheese Dip Recipe

Serving: 10 | Prep: | Cook: 45mins | Ready in:

Ingredients

- 1 cup monterey jack cheese, shredded
- 1 cup cheddar cheese, shredded
- 2 cloves garlic, minced
- 1/4 cup green onions, chopped
- 3 oz. real bacon bits (or cooked crumbled bacon)
- several dashes of Tobasco
- 1 cup sour cream
- 1 tomato, chopped

Direction

- Combine cheeses, garlic, onions, bacon bits and sour cream in a baking dish and mix well. Bake at 350 degrees for 45 minutes. Top with chopped tomato and serve with crackers and/or tortilla chips

50. Hot Broccoli Cheese Dip Recipe

Serving: 8 | Prep: | Cook: 30mins | Ready in:

Ingredients

- 1/2 cup butter
- 6 celery ribs, sliced
- 2 onions, chopped
- 1 1/2 lbs mushrooms, sliced
- 1/4 c. all purpose flour
- 2 cans condensed cream of celery soup (10 oz)
- 6 0z garlic cheese, cut into cubes or cheese of your choice and garlic cloves to your liking
- 2 packages frozen broccoli spears (10 oz)
- -

Direction

- In a large skillet, melt butter. Add celery, onion and mushroom. Cook and stir until translucent. Stir in flour and cook 2 to 3 minutes. Transfer to baking dish.
- Stir in soup, cheese and broccoli. Cover and bake in preheated 350 F oven for 30 minutes. Stir and continue baking for 30 minutes. Serve with French bread slices or crackers.

51. Hot Crab And Cheese Dip Recipe

Serving: 12 | Prep: | Cook: 30mins | Ready in:

Ingredients

- 16 oz claw crab meat
- 8 oz cream cheese room temp
- 1 cup shredded cheese (I like a sharp cheese but use what you like)
- 3 - 6 drops of your favorite hot sauce (you want some heat but not to take over the flavor)
- 1/2 cup chopped raw peeled and devined shrimp
- 1 clove of garlic minced
- 1 tsp Old Bay Seasoning
- 1 tsp onion powder
- 2 tbsp. fresh chopped parsley or 1 tsp dry
- salt and pepper

Direction

- Mix all ingredients in no special order - except to make sure you whip the cream cheese slightly.
- Pour into a well-greased oven safe bowl and bake for 30 mins or until the cheese bubbles up.
- Serve with crostini or warm bread.
- Crostinis are simple slices of your favourite Italian bread (1/4" or less cut on an angle) rubbed with a raw clove of garlic (cut the clove in half and simply rub over each slice of bread) a drizzle of olive oil and a dash of parmesan on each slice. Bake at 325 till golden brown.

52. Hot Fennel Cheese Dip Recipe

Serving: 8 | Prep: | Cook: 20mins | Ready in:

Ingredients

- 4 slices bacon, drained and crumbled
- Save 1 tablespoon bacon grease.**
- 3 medium fennel bulbs, clean and sliced paper thin
- 2 cloves garlic, minced (or more!)
- 8 ounces mayonaise (not Miracle Whip)
- 8 ounces light sour cream
- 4 ounces gorgonzola cheese
- salt and pepper to taste
- Topping:
- 1/4 cup freshly shredded parmesan cheese
- 2 tablespoon finely chopped nuts (or panko if preferred)
- **Use olive oil if desired

Direction

- Sauté fennel slices and garlic in bacon drippings or olive oil
- Mix sautéed veggies with mayonnaise, sour cream, Gorgonzola cheese, salt and pepper.
- Pour mixture in an 8 inch round ceramic baking dish (like the Pampered Chef dish)
- Top with Parmesan cheese mixture.
- Bake at 400 degrees for 15-20 minutes

53. Hot Hot Cheesy Spinach Dip Recipe

Serving: 0 | Prep: | Cook: 4hours | Ready in:

Ingredients

- 2lbs fresh spinach, roughly torn
- 1lb pepper jack cheese, grated
- 8oz Monterey Jack, or other favorite meltable cheese
- 16oz cream cheese
- 1 large(or 2 small) cans water chestnuts diced
- 1 onion, grated
- 3 cloves garlic, minced
- 1T worcestershire sauce
- 1t-1T Tabasco sauce
- kosher or sea salt and plenty of fresh ground pepper
- Couple T of half and half IF NEEDED to thin out finished dip

Direction

- Combine all ingredients in a slow cooker
- Cook on low for several hours, stirring every once in a while to keep ingredients well combined
- Add half and half if needed to thin out the dip once it's finished. I didn't need any. :)
- Remember, spinach will cook down a LOT, so the pot won't be filled once it's ready to serve. :)

54. Hot Spinach And Cheese Dip Recipe

Serving: 6 | Prep: | Cook: 40mins | Ready in:

Ingredients

- 1 package frozen chopped spinach, thawed and as much water removed as possible(squeeze it)
- 1/2 stick butter
- 1 cup sliced green onions
- 2 cloves chopped garlic
- 1 can mild Rotel tomatoes
- 1 cup sour cream
- 4 oz. cream cheese, softened
- 2 pounds Velveeta, cubed

Direction

- Place butter, spinach, garlic, and green onions in crock pot.
- Cook on high heat for 10 to 15 minutes.
- Stir in cream cheese, Rotel, and Velveeta.
- Lower heat and cook for 25 to 30 minutes or until Velveeta is melted.
- Stir in sour cream and continue to cook on low until ready to eat!
- Serve with tortilla chips or corn chips.

55. Hot Bacon And Cheese Dip Recipe

Serving: 8 | Prep: | Cook: 60mins | Ready in:

Ingredients

- 16 slices bacon; cooked crisp and diced
- 2-8 ounce packages cream cheese, softened and cubed
- 4 cups shredded sharp cheddar cheese
- 1 cup half-and-half
- 2 tespoons worcestershire sauce
- 1 teaspoon onion powder
- 1/2 teaspoon garlic powder
- 1/2 teaspoon mustard powder
- 1 teaspoon Frank's Hot Sauce®
- Dipper of your choice

Direction

- Cook bacon to crisp, drain and dice.

- Add all the ingredients to the crock pot.
- Cook on low, stirring occasionally, for about an hour, until cheese is melted.
- Keep on low setting and serve with dippers.

56. Italian Beer Cheese Dip From Mancinos Recipe

Serving: 15 | Prep: | Cook: 35mins | Ready in:

Ingredients

- mayonnaise 1 cup
- beer 1 cup
- ricotta cheese 1 cup
- mozzarella cheese 1 lb.
- cream cheese 8 oz. softened
- pepperoni 12 oz. Cut into strips
- black olives 1 cup sliced
- garlic 1 Tblsp
- **Mancino's seasoning 1 Tblsp
- Italian bread Crumbs
- tortilla chips or toasted Italian bread
- ** Mancino's seasoning Mix : (salt, pepper, garlic, oregano, basil, red pepper flakes) equal parts of each (this is a great seasoning mix, I mix it up by 2 Tablespoons of each, and use until time to mix more!).

Direction

- Combine all ingredients thoroughly place in baking dish
- Sprinkle Italian bread crumbs on top and bake @ 350 for 35-40 minutes
- Serve with Tortilla chips or toasted Italian bread

57. Kenai Alaska Jalepeno Cheese Dip Recipe

Serving: 8 | Prep: | Cook: | Ready in:

Ingredients

- 3 cups shredded chedder cheese
- 1 cup mayo
- 2 fresh jalepenos
- 1/2 tsp cayenne pepper
- 1/2 tsp liquid smoke
- 1 tsp garlic powder
- (optional) pickled jalepeno juice to moisten

Direction

- Place all ingredients in a mixing bowl, stir thoroughly and enjoy.

58. Mexican Cheese Dip Recipe

Serving: 32 | Prep: | Cook: 30mins | Ready in:

Ingredients

- 3 c plain yogurt
- 2 cloves garlic, minced
- 2 tsp ground cumin
- 1/2 tsp seasoned salt
- 1 medium sweet red pepper, diced
- 2 c frozen whole kernel corn, thawed
- 1 c canned black beans, rinsed and drained
- 1 small tomato, seeded and chopped
- 2 Tbs canned diced green chilies
- 2 c shredded Mexican blend cheese
- 1/4 c snipped fresh cilantro
- tortilla chips

Direction

- Line a small colander with 3 layers of cotton cheesecloth or clean paper coffee filter. Suspend colander over a bowl and spoon in yogurt. Cover with plastic wrap and chill overnight to create yogurt cheese.
- Remove yogurt cheese from strainer; discard liquid. Transfer to large bowl. Stir in garlic, cumin, and salt. Fold in sweet pepper, corn black beans, tomato, green chilies, 1-1/2 c shredded cheese and 3 Tbsp. cilantro.
- Spoon into crock or bread bowl or spread on platter. Top with remaining Mexican cheese blend and cilantro. Serve with tortilla chips or crackers.

59. Mexico Chiquito Cheese Dip Recipe

Serving: 6 | Prep: | Cook: 25mins | Ready in:

Ingredients

- 1 stick of butter
- 4 tablespoons flour
- 1 teaspoon paprika
- 1 teaspoon chili powder
- 1 teaspoon cumin seeds
- 1 teaspoon hot pepper sauce
- 1 teaspoon cayenne pepper
- 1/2 teaspoon garlic powder
- 1 tablespoon ketchup
- a dash of salt
- 2 cups milk
- 1 pound Kraft American cheese (the real kind), cut into cubes

Direction

- Melt butter in a saucepan. Add flour and stir around until flour loses its raw taste, about 2 minutes.
- Add the remaining ingredients including the milk.
- Then add the cheese.
- Stir until cheese is melted.
- Serve with tortilla chips.

60. Mikeys Cheese Dip Recipe

Serving: 8 | Prep: | Cook: 20mins | Ready in:

Ingredients

- 1 lb. Velveeta cheese
- 1 10 oz. can of cream of celery soup
- 6 Jalepeno peppers
- 1/2 cup milk
- 1 medium sized onion
- 1/4 stick of butter
- garlic powder (to taste)
- salt (to taste)
- white pepper (to taste)

Direction

- Cut your Velveeta into 1 inch cubes (it will melt so much faster
- Remove the seeds from jalapeños and dice into small pieces.
- In a medium size sauce pan add the butter over LOW heat.
- Sauté onions until translucent.
- Add the soup and milk and cook over low heat.
- Add the Velveeta small amounts at a time until melted completely.
- Add the jalapeños.
- Add Salt, Pepper and Garlic to taste (a pinch of each is what I use)
- Cook over LOW heat stirring often so the mixture does not stick.
- Continue stirring until ready to serve.
- ENJOY, it will go fast I promise!

61. Mozzarella Dip Recipe

Serving: 16 | Prep: | Cook: | Ready in:

Ingredients

- 3 cups shredded mozzarella cheese
- 1 pint mayonnaise
- 1 cup sour cream
- 2 tablespoons parsley flakes
- 1 teaspoon sugar
- 1/2 teaspoon garlic powder
- 1 teaspoon freshly ground black pepper

Direction

- Mix all ingredients in large bowl with mixer.
- Refrigerate overnight to let flavours blend.
- Serve on crackers.

62. Muskoka Goat Cheese Dip Recipe

Serving: 12 | Prep: | Cook: 120mins | Ready in:

Ingredients

- 1 cup olive oil
- 1/3 cup fresh basil (chopped)
- 1/3 cup sun dried tomatoes (chopped)
- 1/4 cup fresh parsley (chopped)
- 1/4 tsp dried thyme
- 1/4 tsp hot pepper flakes
- 1/2 tsp dried rosemary
- 4-5 cloves garlic (minced)
- 2 large goat cheese logs (freeze slightly to slice or just crumble)

Direction

- Crumble or slice cheese into the bottom of serving dish
- Chop all other ingredients and combine in bowl.
- Pour over the goat cheese
- Marinate overnight or at least a couple of hours
- Leave at room temperature for at least 1 hour before serving.
- Serve with sliced baguette or crackers

63. My Own Mexican Cheese Dip Oolala Recipe

Serving: 10 | Prep: | Cook: 10mins | Ready in:

Ingredients

- OKAY HERE GOES!! (Builds your muscles cause you stir alot)
- 1-1/2 pounds Velveeta cheese, cut into 2-inch pieces
- 1/2 stick unsalted butter
- 2 heaping tablespoons flour
- 3/4 cup milk
- 1 can Original Ro-tel tomatoes and green chilies (can use mild or hotter)
- 1 teaspoon ground cumin
- 1/2 teaspoon black pepper
- 1/2 teaspoon garlic powder
- Of course you can make it hotter with more black pepper or red pepper

Direction

- In large bowl, melt butter in microwave, watch it or it will blow! :)
- When melted, remove and add flour, stirring
- Add milk, stir, then add can of Ro-tel, stir
- Add ground cumin, black pepper, and garlic powder, stir
- Return to microwave again for about 1 minute, or more
- Remove, stir, and add cheese
- Return to microwave and cook, watching closely, and removing frequently to stir
- Continue until cheese is melted
- Remove from microwave when it thickens
- Stir again, (see, I told you that you stir a lot!)
- Cheese dip is ready for "dipping" when it is creamy and smooth
- ENJOY, ENJOY
- NOTE: Cumin, black pepper, and garlic powder can be adjusted for individual taste

64. Oh La La Quick Muffalotta Dip Recipe

Serving: 0 | Prep: | Cook: 5mins | Ready in:

Ingredients

- 2 blocks cream cheese. softened
- 1/4 cup shredded parmesan cheese
- 4 to 6 oz. of jarred muffalotta salad mix
- dash cracked pepper
- 2 teaspoons minced garlic
- 1 bunch green onions, sliced
- 1/4 cup chopped baked ham
- 1/4 cup chopped salami
- 1/4 cup chopped or shredded Provolne cheese

Direction

- In a medium or large size mixing bowl, blend together the first 5 ingredients.
- Place in a large serving bowl.
- Decorate top of bowl by placing green onions around bowl, then a layer of ham, a layer of salami and the middle the provolone cheese. Serve with crackers, chips, or my favourite is the Parmesan Wheat Thin triangles!!!
- You can also make this without the meat or the provolone, either way, it is delicious and easy!!!

65. Packer Dip Recipe

Serving: 0 | Prep: | Cook: 2hours | Ready in:

Ingredients

- 16oz cream cheese
- 3 cups shredded colby or cheddar cheese
- 1/2 cup half and half
- 1/4 cup good beer
- 3T Dijon(whole grain or honey dijon would both work well)
- 1 small onion, grated
- 1 clove garlic, minced
- 2t smoked paprika OR 2t sweet paprika and a dash of liquid smoke
- 1T worcestershire sauce
- kosher or sea salt and fresh ground black pepper

- 1lb smoked sausage, chopped(I used specialty sausages, but any of your favorite precooked sausage would do, just don't use partially cooked or raw)
- 2lb baguette, sliced into rounds
- olive oil

Direction

- Combine all ingredients except bread and olive oil, in small crock pot.
- Cook on low for about an hour, stir well, then continue to cook until heated through and completely melted.
- Meanwhile, drizzle bread rounds with olive oil and bake in a 400 oven for about 10-12 minutes or until lightly golden brown around edges.
- Serve dip hot, with bread rounds.

66. Parmesan Artichoke Dip Recipe

Serving: 6 | Prep: | Cook: 30mins | Ready in:

Ingredients

- 4 cloves garlic
- 6 slices pickled jalapeno pepper (or to taste)
- 8 oz. cream cheese, softened
- 4 oz. mayonnaise
- 8 oz. shredded parmesan
- 8 oz. jar artichoke hearts
- 8 oz. crab meat (optional)

Direction

- Preheat oven to 350 degrees (F).
- Mince garlic and jalapeno slices in food processor.
- Add cream cheese, mayonnaise and parmesan and mix well.
- Add artichokes (and crab meat if you're using it) and pulse a few times until mixed but leave some chunks.
- Pour into baking dish and bake at 375 degrees for approximately 20 minutes, or until bubbly and golden brown.
- Let sit for 10 minutes before serving. Dip will firm up as it sits.
- Enjoy!

67. Parmesan Confetti Dip Recipe

Serving: 0 | Prep: | Cook: | Ready in:

Ingredients

- Parmesan Confetti Dip
- Prep Time : 10 min
- Makes: 2-1/3 cups or 20 servings, about 2 tbsp. each
- --
- 1 cup sour cream
- 1/2 cup Grated parmesan cheese
- 1/2 cup Kraft Miracle Whip Dressing
- 1/2 cup each: finely chopped green & red peppers
- 1/2 tsp. garlic powder

Direction

- Mix all ingredients; cover.
- Refrigerate until ready to serve.
- Garnish with additional 1 tsp. chopped peppers, if desired.

68. Parmesan Garlic Rosemary Sicily Italian Bread Dip Mix Seasoning Recipe

Serving: 8 | Prep: | Cook: 8mins | Ready in:

Ingredients

- Sicily

- Italian
- garlic
- rosemary
- parmesan
- olive oil
- www.alabamaspices.com

Direction

- Pour Fresh Olive oil on plate
- Slowly add desired seasoning
- Let air for two minutes and enjoy!

69. Parmesan Salsa Recipe

Serving: 0 | Prep: | Cook: 5mins | Ready in:

Ingredients

- 1/2 pound parmesan, not too dry
- 1/2 pound asiago cheese, not too dry
- 2 teaspoons minced garlic
- 2 teaspoons dried oregano
- 1 teaspoon red pepper flakes
- 2 tablespoons chopped green onion
- 1 1/2 cups extra-virgin olive oil
- 1 teaspoon freshly ground black pepper
- salt to taste

Direction

- Remove any rind from the cheeses and chop the cheeses into rough 1-inch chunks.
- Place the cheese in a food processor with the garlic, oregano, and red pepper flakes and pulse until reduced to the size of fine pea gravel.
- Stir in the green onion, olive oil and black pepper and pulse again. Cover and let stand at room temperature for at least 4 hours before using.

70. Pea Dip With Parmesan Recipe

Serving: 8 | Prep: | Cook: 3mins | Ready in:

Ingredients

- 3 cups peas (frozen are fine)
- 1 cup vegetable stock or water
- 3 Tbs toasted pine nuts
- 1 cup fresh grated parmesan cheese
- 1/2 tsp minced garlic
- 1/4 cup fresh chopped mint or to taste (I prefer cilantro)
- 2 Tbs extra virgin olive oil
- salt and pepper to taste

Direction

- Cook peas with stock or water halfway up to cover them in pan.
- Cook 3 minutes or peas tender and yet bright green
- Put all but one cup of peas in food processor
- Puree, transfer to bowl and stir in remaining peas
- Add nuts, cheese, mint, garlic and olive oil.
- Salt and pepper to taste
- Thin with more liquid if needed to desired consistency
- Variation: 3 cups cooked edamame, 2 Tbsp. miso, 2 Tbsp. water, 1 tbsp. ginger, 1 Tbsp. rice wine vinegar and blend smooth in food processor

71. Potato Dippers With Jalapeno Cheddar Dip Recipe

Serving: 8 | Prep: | Cook: 30mins | Ready in:

Ingredients

- potatoes
- 4 russet potatoes
- 2 tbls. olive oil
- 1/2 tsp. garlic powder

- 1 tsp. chili powder
- Dip
- 1/3 cup sour cream
- 1/3 cup mayonnaise
- 1/4 cup cheddar cheese, shredded
- 1/4 cup tomato, finely chopped
- 2 jalapenos, finely chopped
- 2 scallions, finely sliced for garnish

Direction

- Potatoes
- Preheat oven to 450
- Line large baking sheet with foil
- Spray with cooking spray
- Cut potatoes into thin slices
- Add potatoes, oil, and chili and garlic powder to bowl.
- Coat all potatoes
- Bake for 30 minutes turning over half way through
- Dip
- Mix all dip ingredients except scallions into mixing bowl
- Top with scallions

72. Quick Holiday Cheese Dip Recipe

Serving: 10 | Prep: | Cook: 15mins | Ready in:

Ingredients

- 1 stick butter
- 1 tablespoon minced garlic
- 1 cup sliced green onions
- 1 cup sour cream
- 8 oz. cream cheese, softened
- 1 teaspoon cracked black pepper
- 1 teaspoon dried parsley
- 1/4 cup Frank's hot sauce
- 2 (8 oz) packages shredded cheddar cheese(any variety)
- 4 oz. shredded parmesan cheese
- 1 small can chopped black olives

Direction

- Sauté garlic in butter until lightly browned.
- Mix together cream cheese, garlic butter, green onions, sour cream, pepper, 8 oz. of the shredded cheddar, Parmesan cheese, and hot sauce.
- Spoon into casserole or oven proof serving dish.
- Spread black olives and remaining cheese over top.
- Sprinkle with parsley and bake at 350 degrees for 15 minutes or until lightly browned.
- Serve with assorted chips, crackers, or chunks of toasted French or Italian bread.
- * As an added treat, spread bread with garlic butter and run under broiler until lightly browned before serving with cheese dip.

73. Sausage And Cheese Party Dip Recipe

Serving: 6 | Prep: | Cook: 10mins | Ready in:

Ingredients

- 1/2 pound lean ground beef
- 1/2 pound pork sausage
- 1 pound Velveeta cheese
- 1 cup chopped onion
- 1 cup chunky salsa (Mild, Hot or Hottest -- your choice)
- 1/2 can cream of mushroom soup
- 2 large cloves garlic, minced or put through a garlic press

Direction

- Brown the ground beef and sausage together until crumbly.
- Drain on paper towels to remove as much fat as possible.

- Combine beef/sausage mixture in a heavy saucepan, and add the remaining ingredients.
- Cook and stir over low heat until cheese is melted, and mixture is thoroughly combined.
- Serve warm with tortilla or corn chips.
- Makes 4 to 5 cups.
- Double recipe for a crowd!

74. Sinsinnati Beer Cheese Dip Recipe

Serving: 4 | Prep: | Cook: 5mins | Ready in:

Ingredients

- 3 sharp cheeses, 6 ounces of each; try Asiago, Cheddar, Cooper, Parmesan, Pecorino Romano or Manchego
- 1-1/2 ounces Roquefort cheese
- 2 tablespoons butter
- 2 garlic cloves, minced
- 1 medium onion, finely diced
- 1 teaspoon worcestershire sauce
- hot sauce to taste
- 1 cup dark beer

Direction

- In a mixing bowl, with an electric mixer, mix together all the cheese, butter, garlic, onion, Worcestershire sauce and hot sauce.
- In a small saucepan, warm the beer but not to a boil.
- Gradually add the warm beer to the cheese mixture and mix until of good dipping consistency.
- Cover and refrigerate 1 hour before serving.
- Really cheesy and flavourful spread for crackers!

75. Slow Cooker Cheese Dip Recipe

Serving: 1618 | Prep: | Cook: 120mins | Ready in:

Ingredients

- 1 lb 95% lean ground beef
- 1 lb bulk Italian sausage
- 16 oz pasteurized processed cheese (Velveta), cubed
- 11 oz can sliced jalapeno peppers, drained
- 1 medium onion, diced
- 8 oz cheddar cheese, cubed
- 8 oz cream cheese, cubed
- 8 oz cottage cheese
- 8 oz sour cream
- 8 oz can diced tomatoes, drained
- 3 cloves of garlic, minced
- Dash of salt and pepper

Direction

- Brown ground beer and sausage in skillet over medium-high heat, stirring to break up meat. Drain and discard fat.
- Transfer meat and all other ingredients to crock-pot slow cooker.
- Cover and cook on high for 1 1/2 to 2 hours or until cheeses melted. Do not open the cover until finished.
- Serve with crackers or tortilla chips.

76. Southwestern Cheese Dip Recipe

Serving: 12 | Prep: | Cook: 30mins | Ready in:

Ingredients

- 2 lbs Velveeta, cubed
- 1/2 stick of butter
- 1 green bell pepper
- 3 cloves minced garlic
- 1 onion, chopped

- 2 cups diced (cut into small pieces or shredded) cooked chicken
- 1 can chopped green chilies
- 1 package mild taco seasoning
- 1 1/2 cups mild or medium chunky style salsa
- juice from 2 limes

Direction

- Cook onions, garlic, and bell pepper in butter until tender.
- Place all ingredients in crock pot and cook on high heat for 15 minutes.
- Lower heat and cook until cheese is melted.
- Serve with favourite chips and side of sour cream.
- Extra limes on the side if desired.

77. Spicey Sausage Cream Cheese Dip Recipe

Serving: 10 | Prep: | Cook: 12mins | Ready in:

Ingredients

- 2 packages cream cheese (room temp)
- 1 lb package Hot pork sausage
- 1 can Original Rotel tomatoes w/ green Chiles
- 3 green onions Chopped
- 2 cloves garlic minced
- Frito's Scoops

Direction

- Place Cream Cheese in a small crock pot and turn on low.
- Cook Sausage until browned in a heavy skillet, over med high. When sufficiently browned, drain Sausage and add Green Onion and Garlic and cook 2 minutes more.
- Add the Rotel Tomatoes w/ Green Chiles. Stir until mixture is hot and bubbling.
- Add Hot Sausage mixture to the crock pot with Cream Cheese.
- Mix well.
- Keep on low setting and serve with Frito's Scoops

78. Spinach With Feta Cheese Dip Recipe

Serving: 8 | Prep: | Cook: 10mins | Ready in:

Ingredients

- 2 cups sour cream
- 1 package frozen chopped spinach
- 1/4 pound feta cheese cubed
- 1 garlic clove diced and crushed
- 1 tablespoon dill seed

Direction

- Place sour cream in medium bowl.
- Cook spinach according to package directions and drain thoroughly.
- Stir spinach into sour cream then add remaining ingredients stirring gently.

79. String Cheese Sticks With Dipping Sauce Recipe

Serving: 4 | Prep: | Cook: 10mins | Ready in:

Ingredients

- 2-1/4 cups original Bisquick
- 2/3 cup milk
- 1 pkg (8 ounces) plain or smoked string cheese
- 1 tablespoon butter or margarine, ..melted
- 1/4 teaspoon garlic powder
- 1 can (8 ounces) pizza sauce, heated

Direction

- Preheat oven to 450 degrees F.

- Stir Bisquick and milk until a soft dough forms; beat 30 seconds with a spoon.
- Place dough on surface sprinkled with Bisquick; gently roll in Bisquick to coat.
- Shape into a ball; knead 10 times
- Roll dough 1/4 inch thick.
- Cut into 8 - 6 x 2 inch rectangles
- Roll each rectangle around 1 piece of cheese, pinch edge into roll and seal; seal ends...roll on surface to completely enclose cheese sticks. Place seam sides down on ungreased cookie sheet.
- Bake 8 to 10 minutes or until golden brown;
- Mix butter and garlic powder, and brush over warm cheese sticks, before removing from cookie sheet.
- Serve warm with pizza sauce for dip or you can use a ranch dip

80. Supposedly Wilt Chamberlins Hot Cheese Spinach Dip Recipe

Serving: 6 | Prep: | Cook: 10mins | Ready in:

Ingredients

- 1 package of chopped spinach, defrosted and squeezed dry
- 1 cup of chicken stock
- fresh ground black pepper, more pepper, more better
- 4 to 6 dashes of your favorite hot sauce (Texas Pete here)
- 1 cup each of three white cheeses, your choice as long as one of them is white cheddar.
- 1 1/2 tsp of cornstarch tossed with each cup of white cheese
- 1 cup of half and half
- 2 tsp of garlic powder

Direction

- Heat the stock in the top half of a double boiler, add the hot sauce, garlic powder, black pepper and stir in the spinach.
- Keep stirring and add handful of each cheese that was tossed with the cornstarch.
- Stir slowly until each handful melts.
- Stir in cream, heat gently.
- Adjust seasoning for spiciness, adjust to taste.
- Serve with bread cubes, pretzel rods, blanched veggies; whatever floats your boat.

81. Three Cheese Spinach Artichoke Dip Recipe

Serving: 8 | Prep: | Cook: 30mins | Ready in:

Ingredients

- Three cheese spinach artichoke Dip
- 1-8 oz frozen spinach w/ out any sauce
- 1-8 oz Shredded Three or Four cheese Italian blend (Parmesan, Mozzarella, Provolone, optional Asiago)
- 1-16 oz Bottle/can of ready made alfredo sauce or homemade (see Recipe below)
- 1-8 oz. Can of chopped artichokes in water (NOT marinated in oil)
- salt & pepper to taste
- Homemade alfredo sauce
- 2-3 cloves of minced garlic (depending on how garlic you like the sauce)
- 1 pint of heavy whipping cream
- 2 tablespoons of butter
- 1½ cups of grated parmesan cheese
- salt and pepper to taste

Direction

- Dip:
- 1. Preheat Oven to 375 degrees.
- 2. Open, drain, and roughly chop Artichokes.
- 3. In a casserole dish combine/mix drained artichokes, thawed (squeeze excess water) frozen spinach, Alfredo sauce (see below for homemade recipe), and half of the bag of shredded cheese.
- 4. Top off the dip with the rest of the shredded cheese

- 5. bake for 30 minutes or until dip is hot and all of the cheese has melted.
- Alfredo Sauce
- 1. In a medium saucepan combine the heavy whipping cream, butter and minced garlic.
- 2. Once the mixture has begun to simmer add Parmesan cheese and stir consistently until the texture is creamy.
- 3. If mixture doesn't thicken up add a ¼ teaspoon of flour and continue to stir until mixture coats the spoon.
- 4. Add salt and pepper to taste.

82. Vidalia Onion Cheese Dip Recipe

Serving: 4 | Prep: | Cook: 25mins | Ready in:

Ingredients

- 3 large Vadalia onions, coarsely chopped
- 2 Tbsp. margarine
- 8-ounces sharp cheddar cheese, grated
- 1 cup mayonnaise
- 1/2 teaspoon Tabasco sauce
- 1 clove garlic, minced or a few shakes of garlic powder
- tortilla chips or crackers

Direction

- Preheat oven to 375 degrees. Sauté onions in margarine. Mix cheese, mayonnaise, garlic and Tabasco sauce. Stir in onions. Put in buttered casserole and cook 25 minutes. Serve hot with tortilla chips or crackers.

83. Warm Blue Cheese Bacon Garlic Dip Recipe

Serving: 6 | Prep: | Cook: 40mins | Ready in:

Ingredients

- 7 slices bacon, chopped
- 2 cloves garlic, minced
- 8 ounces cream cheese, softened
- 1/4 cup half and half
- 4 ounces blue cheese, crumbled
- 2 tabs chopped fresh chives
- 3 tabs chopped smoked almonds

Direction

- 1- Cook bacon in a large skillet over medium-high until almost crisp, about 7 minutes.
- 2- Drain excess fat from skillet. Add garlic and cook until bacon is crisp, about 3 minutes.
- 3- Preheat oven to 350 degrees. Beat cream cheese until smooth. Add half and half and mix until combined. Stir in bacon mixture, blue cheese, and chives.
- 4- Transfer to a 2- cup ovenproof serving dish and cover with foil. Bake until thoroughly heated, about 30 minutes. Sprinkle with chopped almonds.
- 5- May be prepared 1 day in advance. Keep refrigerated, if going to a party. Bake it there.

84. Warm Blue Cheese Dip Recipe

Serving: 10 | Prep: | Cook: 30mins | Ready in:

Ingredients

- 8 slices hickory smoked bacon, diced
- 2 cloves garlic, minced
- 8 oz cream cheese, softened
- 1/4 c heavy cream
- 4 oz crumbled blue cheese (1 c)
- 2 Ths chopped fresh chives
- 2 Tbs chopped almonds
- chopped fresh parsley
- crackers, French bread and/or fresh vegetables

Direction

- Preheat oven to 350 degrees. In non-stick skillet, cook bacon over medium-high heat for about 8 mins or till nearly crisp.
- Drain bacon; wipe skillet dry. Return bacon to skillet; add garlic and cook over medium heat till bacon is crisp, about 3 mins, making sure garlic doesn't burn. Drain on paper towels.
- With mixer on medium speed, beat cream cheese until smooth. Add cream; beat well. Fold in bacon, garlic, blue cheese and chives.
- Transfer to 2 cup baking dish. Sprinkle top evenly with almonds. Bake until heated through and browned on top, 25-30 mins.
- Sprinkle with parsley. Serve with crackers, bread and/or vegetables.

85. Warm Crab Parmesan Dip Recipe

Serving: 20 | Prep: | Cook: 45mins | Ready in:

Ingredients

- 1 (6 ounce) can crabmeat, drained and flaked
- 1 (8 ounce) package cream cheese, softened
- 1 cup mayonnaise
- 1 1/2 cups grated parmesan cheese
- 1 cup sour cream
- 4 cloves garlic, peeled and crushed

Direction

- Preheat oven to 350 degrees F (175 degrees C).
- In a small baking dish, mix the crabmeat, cream cheese, mayonnaise, Parmesan cheese, sour cream and garlic.
- Bake uncovered in the preheated oven 45 minutes, or until bubbly and lightly browned.

86. Warm Crab Spinach And Parmesan Dip Recipe

Serving: 0 | Prep: | Cook: 15mins | Ready in:

Ingredients

- 2 tbsp. butter
- 2 tbsp. olive oil
- 1 1/4 cups finely chopped onion
- 1/2 cup chopped green onion
- 6 large garlic cloves, minced
- 2 tbsp. all purpose flour
- 1/2 cup chicken stock
- 1/2 cup whipping cream
- 1 can crab meat, drained, picked over
- 1 10 oz. pkg. frozen spinach, thawed and squeezed dry
- 1 cup grated parmesan cheese
- 1/4 cup sour cream
- 1/2 tsp. cayenne pepper
- toasted baguette slices

Direction

- Melt butter with oil in heavy pot over medium heat.
- Add onions and garlic; sauté until onion is tender, do not brown, about 6 minutes.
- Add flour; stir 2 minutes. Gradually whisk in stock and cream; bring to boil, whisking constantly. Cook until mixture thickens, stirring frequently.
- Remove from heat. Stir in crab, spinach, cheese, sour cream and cayenne. Season with salt and pepper.
- Transfer to serving bowl. Serve warm with toasted baguette slices.

87. Warm Havarti Spinach Dip Recipe

Serving: 8 | Prep: | Cook: 5mins | Ready in:

Ingredients

- 8 ounces cream cheese softened
- 10 ounce package frozen creamed spinach thawed
- 2 cups havarti cheese cubed
- 1 teaspoon garlic powder

Direction

- Beat cream cheese until smooth in medium bowl then stir in remaining ingredients.
- Microwave on high for 5 minutes stirring once during cooking.
- Serve with crackers or bread slices.

88. Zesty Chili Cheese Dip Recipe

Serving: 15 | Prep: | Cook: 240mins | Ready in:

Ingredients

- 1 medium onion, finely chopped
- 2 garlic cloves, minced
- 2 teaspoons vegetable oil
- 2 cans chili without beans (15 ounces each)
- 2 cups salsa
- 2 packages cream cheese, cubed (3 oz each)
- 2 cans olives, sliced and drained (2 1/4 each)

Direction

- In a skillet, sauté onion and garlic in oil until tender.
- Transfer to a slow cooker.
- Stir in the chili, salsa, cream cheese, and olives
- Cover and cook on low for 4 hours or until heated thoroughly, stirring occasionally.
- This makes about 6 cups of dip.
- Serve with tortilla chips...

Index

A
Artichoke 3,4,15,17,20,27,32

B
Bacon 3,4,7,8,10,21,23,33
Basil 3,16
Beer 3,4,8,23,30
Bread 3,8,27
Brie 3,13
Broccoli 3,21
Butter 15

C
Cheddar 3,11,12,28,30
Cheese 1,3,4,5,6,7,8,9,10,12,13,14,15,16,17,18,19,20,21,22,23,24,25,26,29,30,31,32,33,35
Chicken 3,11
Cola 3,14
Crab 3,4,14,21,34
Cream 3,4,15,16,31
Crostini 22
Crumble 20,25
Cumin 26

D
Dijon mustard 11

F
Fennel 3,22
Feta 3,4,5,11,17,18,31
French bread 15,21,33

G
Garlic 1,3,4,5,7,14,18,25,27,31,33
Gorgonzola 22
Guacamole 3,15

J
Jus 5,17

L
Lemon 3,12,16

M
Manchego 30
Milk 14
Mince 12,27
Mozzarella 3,25,32

N
Nut 3,18

O
Oil 3,12
Olive 3,12,28
Onion 3,4,12,31,33

P
Parmesan 3,4,16,20,22,26,27,28,29,30,32,33,34
Parsley 15
Pecorino 30
Peel 6,16
Pepper 16,25
Port 10
Potato 3,16,28,29

R
Roquefort 14,30
Rosemary 3,27

S

Salsa 3,28

Salt 12,16,25,28

Sausage 3,4,29,31

Seasoning 3,21,27

Spinach 3,4,20,22,31,32,34

T

Tabasco 14,16,22,33

Tea 16

Tomato 31

W

Worcestershire sauce 8,9,14,30

Z

Zest 4,35

Conclusion

Thank you again for downloading this book!

I hope you enjoyed reading about my book!

If you enjoyed this book, please take the time to share your thoughts and post a review on Amazon. It'd be greatly appreciated!

Write me an honest review about the book – I truly value your opinion and thoughts and I will incorporate them into my next book, which is already underway.

Thank you!

If you have any questions, **feel free to contact at:** *author@rosemaryrecipes.com*

Jennifer Allen

rosemaryrecipes.com

Printed in Great Britain
by Amazon